Celebrates one of the largest carnivals.

Every year I like to go to the biggest Carnival.

It is called Mardi Gras.

Mardi Gras is celebrated on "Fat Tuesday".

Mardi is the French word for "Tuesday".

Gras is the French word for "Fat".

Mardi Gras colors are purple, gold, and green.

Green is Faith
Gold is Power
Purple is Justice

Mardi Gras is a holiday that dates back thousands of years.

The First American Mardi Gras took place when the French Explorers landed near New Orleans, Louisiana.

Mardi Gras is celebrated in many countries' around the world Brazil, Venice, and New Orleans.

Mardi Gras is the holiday celebrated with street parties.

King of Carnival is named.

Queen of Carnival.

Kings and Queens wear colorful costumes and danced through the streets of New Orleans.

The King and Queen celebrate with friends at a Carnival Ball.

And enjoy fancy dinners.

Decorate a float for the festival parade.

With marching bands
and rolling floats.

You throw beads to people at the parade.

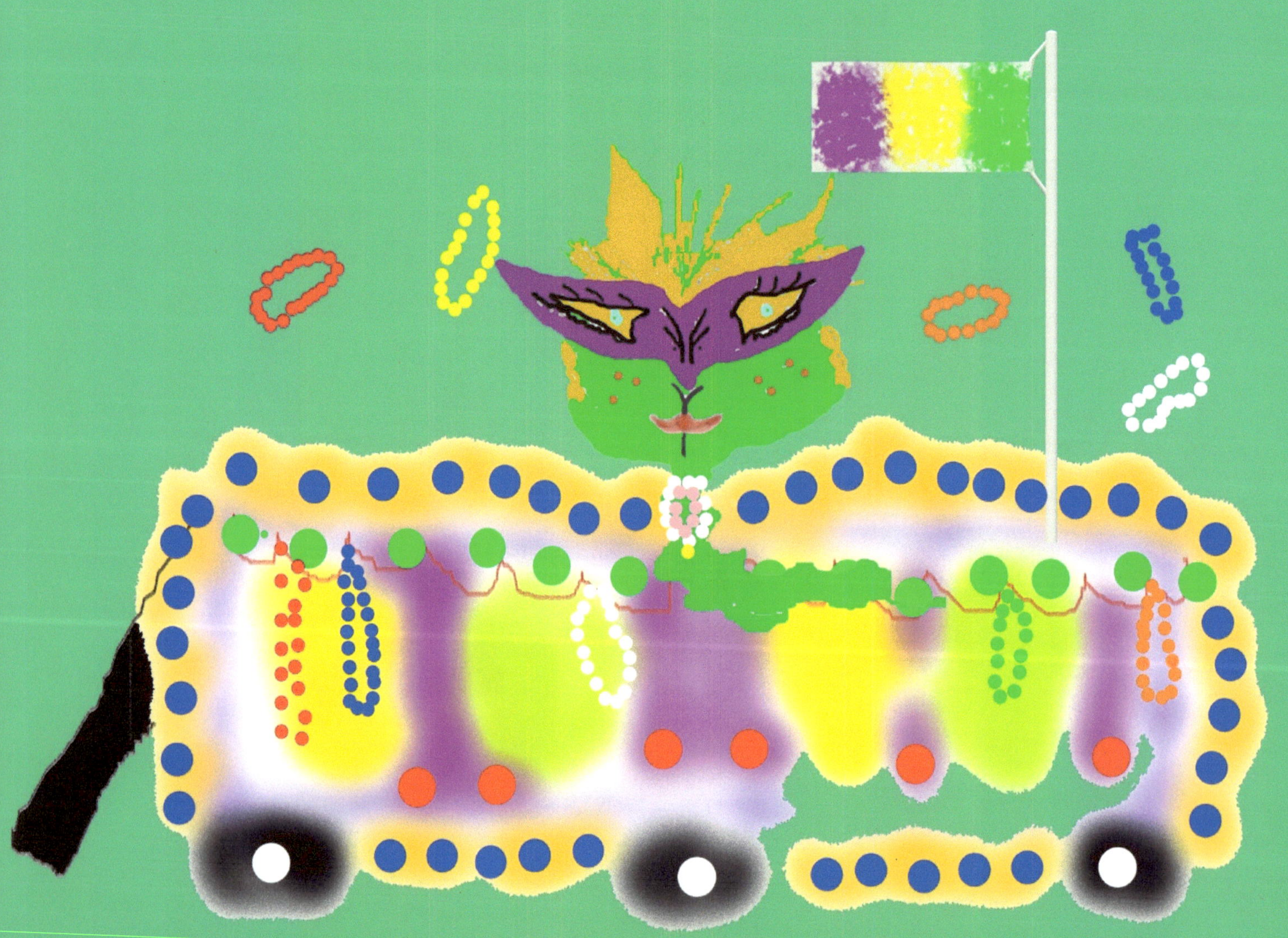

Shiny, colorful bead necklaces are called "Throws".

People line up to catch as many beaded necklaces.

They catch
large coins
called,
"doubloons."

Feathered masks are popular.

Everyone likes to eat Mardi
Gras King Cake.

A baby toy is than hidden inside of the cake.

Whoever has the toy baby in their slice of cake would buy king cake for the next party.

<u>Here are 8 tips to enjoy and be safe for a parade:</u>

1: Plan ahead,
2: Bring snacks,
3: Bring a stroller or a wagon,
4: Change of clothing,
5: Pack for the weather,
6: Go in a group,
7: Do not run into the street for the candy,
8: Do not forget sunscreen and water.